D1325963

preserves

JAMS, PICKLES AND LIQUEURS

preserves

JAMS, PICKLES AND LIQUEURS

LINDY WILDSMITH

PHOTOGRAPHY BY TARA FISHER

RYLAND
PETERS
& SMALL

LONDON NEW YORK

Senior Designer	Paul Tilby
Commissioning Editor	Elsa Petersen-Schepelern
Production	Patricia Harrington
Art Director	Gabriella Le Grazie
Publishing Director	Alison Starling
Food Stylist	Bridget Sargeson
Props Stylist	Chloe Brown

First published in Great Britain in 2004

10 9 8 7 6 5 4 3 2 1

by Ryland Peters & Small
Kirkman House
12–14 Whitfield Street
London W1T 2RP

Text © Lindy Wildsmith 2004
Design and photographs ©
Ryland Peters & Small 2004

Printed and bound in China

ISBN 1 84172 714 8

A CIP record for this book is available
from the British Library

STERILIZATION OF PRESERVING JARS

Wash the jars in hot, soapy water and rinse in boiling water. Place in a large saucepan and then cover with hot water. With the lid on, bring the water to the boil and continue boiling for 15 minutes. Turn off the heat, then leave the jars in the hot water until just before they are to be filled. Invert the jars onto a clean kitchen towel to dry. Sterilize the lids for 5 minutes, by boiling, or according to the manufacturer's instructions. Alternatively, follow the advice on page 7. Jars should be filled and sealed while they are still hot.

The size and shape of jars are often dictated by the type of preserve you are making. Large jars with wide necks are needed for packing whole fruits, whereas smaller ones, 250–500 ml, are more useful for jellies, chutneys, conserves, etc.

NOTES

All spoon measurements are level unless otherwise stated.

CONTENTS

introduction

When you get into the swing of preserving, it can be a lot of fun, but it can be frustrating – like when your jam doesn't set straight away. So don't rush it – take your time. It will come right in the end. When you have mastered the basic recipes, it is simplicity itself, but the temptation to preserve every fruit and vegetable in sight becomes irresistible.

If you don't grow your own, preserving can be expensive, even at 'pick your own' and farm gate prices. However, the sheer pleasure makes it all worthwhile. Your work sits on the shelf seductively maturing, promising the taste and essence of summer in every pot.

Jams are made with whole fruit, marmalades with the zest of citrus fruit and jellies with the juice of the fruit. Pickles and chutneys are made with fruit and vegetables and preserved in all kinds of vinegars. Fruit can also be preserved in spirits as an after-dinner treat, in vinegar to create interesting pickles, salted for use in cooking, or made into liqueurs.

If you can bear the wait, leave your jam and chutney to mature for at least a month, while pickles are best kept for three months. Liqueurs, I'm afraid, should be left for at least twelve months.

My native Britain is famous for fine preserves, teas and porcelain and the history of all three is intertwined. The Museum of Worcester Porcelain has a fascinating collection of early (around 1760) blue-and-white, leaf-shaped, underglaze pickle dishes. This was not culinary affectation - they were made because the vinegar in pickles attacked other porcelain finishes.

Pickle dishes were made in sets and sat ceremoniously in the centre of the table to accommodate the wide range of sweet and savoury pickles so popular at the time, not least of all to pep up otherwise dreary food. Each place setting had its own dish, just as they do today in an Indian or Chinese restaurant.

GENERAL PRESERVING EXPLAINED

EQUIPMENT: You need a large pan, wooden spoon, ladle, clean jars with lids, a pack of paper covers with elastic bands, waxed discs and labels. A spice bag for flavourings and a skimmer would be useful too. A stainless steel preserving pan is essential for making large quantities. A sugar thermometer may also be useful as would a jam funnel – though I have neither. For jellies, you need a jelly bag. You can buy special stands for them, but I use an S-hook suspended from a cupboard door handle.

FRUIT AND VEGETABLES: Choose only good-quality, dry produce in peak condition. Do not use over-ripe fruit. If you grow your own, use produce as it matures, not when it is past its best. Windfall hard fruits can be used, as long as you cut away the bruised parts. After you have mastered the basics, you can experiment with all kinds of produce, spices, herbs and nuts.

QUANTITIES: Before refrigeration, preserving was the only means of bringing variety to the table out of season. As recently as the 1950s and 60s, thrifty people grew produce in gardens and allotments to make preserves to keep them going through the winter. Old recipes were for large quantities, but you can use as little as 500 g of fruit and sugar. This will make only a pot or two, but it won't take long to prepare, cook and set. Transfer the scrapings of the jam pan to a small dish to sample on toast for breakfast the following morning (cook's perks). If it hasn't set, it will not be too late to boil it up again.

JARS: Keep a plentiful supply of jars and lids ready for use. Sizes are many and confusing. Smaller 390 ml and 200 ml jars are good for jams, small pickles and chutneys and 500 g jars for preserved and pickled fruits.

HYGIENE: For home consumption, all equipment should be washed in a dishwasher or in fresh, hot, soapy water. Jars and lids should be blemish free. Arrange the clean jars on a baking tray in a cool oven – 110°C (225°F) Gas ¼ – until heated. Pouring hot preserves into cold jars will make them crack. Alternatively, sterilize as described on page 4. To sterilize lids, boil for 5 minutes or according to the manufacturer's instructions. When your preserve is ready, it should be potted quickly, covered and sealed. Most preserves have a very long shelf life until opened. After opening, store in a cool place and use quickly.

POTTING AND SEALING: Fill the warmed jars from a ladle or jug. Jellies are potted at once. Jams and marmalades containing whole fruit or pieces of fruit must stand in the pan for 20–30 minutes, stirred well to distribute the fruit, then potted. Fill the jars to the neck. Cover the preserve with a waxed disc (shiny side down), taking care not to create bubbles between the preserve and the paper (because this would encourage mould). Wipe the neck with a clean, damp cloth. While still hot, seal with a lid or cover

and elastic band. Wipe and let cool, label with date and contents, then store in a cool, dark cupboard.

FINISHING TOUCHES

Whether your preserves are for yourself or for gifts, they need a little titivating. Collect fabric remnants and funky papers to tie over the lids –18 cm squares at most – plus a pair of pinking shears to finish the edges. You can write on paper covers to eliminate labels. Lengths of string, twine, cord, ribbon, thread, wire or wool make good ties, but use an elastic band as well for use after the jar has been opened. If the jars have plain metal lids, cut out motifs and glue on.

JAM, JELLY and MARMALADE MAKING EXPLAINED

PECTIN: All fruit contains pectin in the cell walls and it is this pectin that sets preserves. Apples and lemons are pectin-rich, strawberries and blackberries are pectin-poor, while other fruits stand somewhere in the middle. Apple jelly sets very well, blackberry jelly does not – combine the two and you will have a really good set. Equally, mix strawberries and lemon juice and your jam will set well. If in doubt about the level of pectin in your fruit, simply add the juice of half a lemon to every 500 g of fruit. Acidity also helps the set and an acid note will add a sharp edge to the sweet flavour of the jams. Commercially produced pectin can be added for a thick set (follow the packet instructions). However, I prefer the natural set created by pectin-rich fruit.

The pectin level in fruit is at its highest when the fruit is only just ripe and still firm; pectin diminishes the riper the fruit. This is why it is essential to use fruit in peak condition, slightly under-ripe rather than over-ripe.

PRE-COOKING THE FRUIT: Soft fruits such as raspberries, blackberries and strawberries require little pre-cooking but fruit such as apricots, plums, figs, pears and apples should be simmered gently in water until soft before adding the sugar. The longer you cook the fruit, the softer it becomes and if you do not like whole fruit in your jam, simply mash the cooked fruit to reduce it to pulp. Remember the more water added to the fruit, the longer the reduction time.

SUGAR: Should be added over very low heat, then stirred into the fruit until dissolved, otherwise it will go hard and burn. Preserving sugar dissolves quicker, but I find regular sugar works just as well, although you may prefer to use preserving sugar for marmalades and jellies. If you warm the sugar first, it will dissolve quicker.

SETTING: When the fruit is soft, the water reduced and sugar dissolved, increase the heat and boil hard. At first the bubbles will be small, white and frothy, but as the liquid reduces, the bubbles become larger and the fruit colour starts to show though. When the bubbles have a caramel appearance, setting point is near.

TESTING FOR SET: Before you start jam making, always put a saucer and 2–3 teaspoons in the refrigerator or freezer to cool. Boil the reduced preserve hard for 5 minutes, then take the pan off the heat and test for set. Take a teaspoon of the preserve, put it on the cold saucer in the refrigerator or freezer and leave for 5 minutes. Push it with a finger – if it offers resistance or crinkles, it is ready. If, on the other hand, it is still liquid, simply return the pan to the heat, boil a few minutes longer and test again. Do not leave the pan boiling while testing. The jam will overcook, become caramelized, sticky, lose its colour or even burn. Just be patient, pull the pan off the heat and wait a few minutes.

Alternatively use a sugar thermometer to gauge setting point – 110°C (224°F).

SKIMMING: Scum forms on jams and jellies during boiling. Don't remove it until setting point has been reached and the heat turned off. Scum keeps forming during cooking, so do it once at the end. Use a flat, perforated skimmer.

YIELD: It is quite difficult to be accurate as to how much preserve you will end up with – 500 g of fruit tends to yield 500–750 g of jam, more marmalade and less jelly. It's impossible to judge, so be flexible.

AN EXTRA NOTE FOR JELLY MAKERS

Jellies are made with the juice of fruits simmered in water, then drained in a jelly bag overnight. It is tempting to stint on the water – many recipes suggest using pure fruit juice. However this can produce a very disappointing yield.

Scald the jelly bag with boiling water before adding the fruit. The fabric then absorbs water, not juice. Never squeeze the bag, because this will cause the jelly to cloud. Instead, leave it to drip naturally overnight.

When drained, simply measure the juice and add 450 g sugar to every 600 ml juice. Apples and crab-apples yield well and make easy jellies for a first experiment.

WHAT CAN GO WRONG

The most common fault with jam and jelly making is not getting a good set. If you discover after potting that your jam has not quite set, don't worry. When you have half an hour to spare, return the jam to the pan, boil it again slowly, then boil hard for a few minutes and test for set. You must of course wash the jars and lids again and use fresh wax discs when re-potting.

If a tiny piece of fruit catches on the bottom of the pan, take it out and continue, if more has caught, transfer the jam to a clean pan and continue.

If the jam crystallizes, it is because you boiled the sugar before it dissolved or you used too much sugar. There is nothing to do but start again.

If you over-boil jam and it becomes hard and sticky or burns – forget it.

PRESERVED FRUITS EXPLAINED

There are many ways of preserving whole fruit, but here
I deal only with the use of spirits, vinegars and spices,
which are all natural preservatives.

There are many kinds of jars available from 100 ml
to 3–4 litre capacities – follow the manufacturer's
instructions. However, because the recipes in this chapter
use spirits or vinegar to preserve the fruit, jars do not need
sterilizing after filling.

If stems are still attached to pears, cherries, plums , or
other fruits, preserve them as well. Tuck whole spices such
as star anise on the outside of the fruit where it shows
through the glass – this will give your preserves a professional
look. Preserved fruits keep well for 6 months to a year, but
once opened must be eaten immediately. So don' t be
tempted to peek.

LIQUEUR MAKING EXPLAINED

There is fun and magic in liqueur making, evoking both
childhood games and the alchemist's art. There is little
preparation, simply steeping and shaking the fruit with
spirits and sugar, then waiting at least 12 months until
your brew is perfectly matured. Use any colourless spirit,
such as gin, rum or vodka – or brandy.

Liqueurs were once highly regarded not only as drinks, but
also as medicines and every household had its secret recipe.
They are served after a meal because they aid digestion.

EQUIPMENT: You will need a ready supply of large, clean
glass jars with screwtop lids for steeping the fruit, a large
plastic funnel, a packet of large coffee filter papers, a
mortar and pestle, a jelly bag, a selection of interesting
screwtop or corked bottles and adhesive labels – and of
course an elegant decanter and glasses.

PICKLE and CHUTNEY MAKING EXPLAINED

Pickles are fruit and vegetables preserved in vinegar and
spices. Chutneys are chopped, cooked slowly with vinegar
and spices and packed closely into jars. Push pickles down
with the handle of a wooden spoon, then top up with
vinegar. Check jars for air bubbles before sealing; simply
slide a clean knife blade down the side of the jar to release
them. Raw fruit and vegetable pickles should be kept at
least 3 months before opening. Cooked pickles and chutney
may be eaten after 1 month. After opening, pickles should
be used quickly.

JAMS, JELLIES AND MARMALADES

e sure to read Jam, Jelly and Marmalade Making explained (page 7) before starting a recipe.

Dried apricot conserve

Apricots make one of the most luxurious preserves of all, and it can be made with dried as well as fresh apricots. Dried apricots need soaking well, then long, slow cooking to soften them. The apricot season is fairly short and if, like me, you love apricots and find it difficult to resist eating them, you might find this recipe using dried apricots very useful.

500 g dried apricots (soaked weight 1 kg)

freshly squeezed juice of 1 lemon

1 kg sugar

50 g walnut halves broken into 4 pieces

2 tablespoons Amaretto liqueur (optional)

4 clean, dry, warm jam jars, 250 g each, with lids or covers

waxed paper discs

MAKES ABOUT 1 KG

Cut the apricots in half, put in a large bowl, cover with cold water, add the lemon juice and set aside for 24 hours.

Strain off the juice into a measuring jug and make up to 1 litre with cold water.

Put the fruit in a heavy pan, add the juice and water and simmer over low heat for 30 minutes or until quite soft. The fruit can be mashed at this stage or left in pieces.

Add the sugar and bring slowly to simmering point. Cook gently, stirring until dissolved.

Increase the heat and boil hard for 10 minutes, add the walnut pieces and return to a fast boil.

Slide the pan off the heat and let stand while you test for set (page 8). If the jam is not ready, put the pan back on the heat to boil for a few minutes longer and test again. Repeat this process if necessary and remember to take the jam off the heat while testing, because over-boiling will ruin it.

When setting point has been reached, add the Amaretto to the pan, return to the boil, stir and skim if necessary. Let the jam rest for 20 minutes, then stir well and ladle into jars, Seal at once with waxed paper discs and lids or covers. Let cool, label and store in a cool, dark cupboard until required.

VARIATION **Fresh apricot preserve**

Cut 1 kg fresh apricots into small pieces, remove the stones, but do not discard. Put the fruit in a pan, add 150 ml water and the lemon juice and cook until quite soft. Crack 12 apricot stones and take out the kernels. Blanch the kernels in boiling water, remove the skins and pat dry. Proceed as for the main recipe, adding the apricot kernels instead of the walnuts.

Dolly's strawberry jam

Dolly Nash was an old family friend, 'a county woman' as my Mother liked to call her, even though she came from far-away Tasmania. As a child in the 1950s, I loved visiting her picture-book farmhouse – the low-ceilinged bedrooms and high beds with feather mattresses were straight out of a fairy story, as was Dolly's Strawberry Jam.

1 kg small strawberries, picked in dry weather

freshly squeezed juice of 1 lemon

1 kg sugar

4 clean, dry, warm jam jars, 250 g each, with lids or covers

waxed paper discs

MAKES ABOUT 1 KG

Wash the fruit if necessary and pat dry. Hull the strawberries and discard any that are not in perfect condition. Put in a large pan and cook gently over very low heat just for a few minutes to start the juices running. Take care not to let the fruit burn. Let stand overnight. If you like, the fruit can be mashed at this stage.

Add the lemon juice and sugar to the fruit and bring to simmering point over low heat. Stir well while the sugar is dissolving. When the sugar has dissolved, increase the heat and boil rapidly for 10 minutes (remember to stir occasionally to make sure the pan does not burn), until the juice has reduced and the jam starts to thicken.

Take the pan off the heat and test for set (page 8). If the jam is not ready, put the pan back on the heat to boil for a few minutes longer and test again. Repeat this process if necessary and remember to take the jam off the heat while testing, because over-boiling will ruin it.

When setting point has been reached, skim the jam with a perforated skimmer, stir it well and let stand for 20 minutes for the fruit to settle. Stir and ladle into clean, dry, warm jars. Seal at once with waxed paper discs, wiping the necks of the jars with a clean, damp cloth if necessary. Close with a lid or appropriate cover.

Let cool, label and store in a cool, dark cupboard until required.

VARIATION **Strawberry jam with balsamic vinegar**

If you have a taste for strawberries with balsamic vinegar, here is a foolproof, grown-up recipe. I love it on toast for breakfast or with scones and cream, but it also makes wonderful little tarts topped with whipped cream, or try it melted on ice cream.

Follow the instructions for the main recipe, but omit the lemon juice and, rather than cooking the fruit first, put it in a bowl, add the sugar and 150 ml balsamic vinegar, cover with a clean cloth and let steep overnight. Stir from time to time.

Italian fig conserve

Traditionally, Italian jams are made with slightly less sugar than other jams; say eight parts sugar to ten parts fruit, rather than the usual equal parts. This is because peaches, apricots, figs and other typically Mediterranean fruits are sweet compared with temperate soft fruits and plums, which are acidic and require more sugar.

Make sure you use only plump, firm fruit. You can use green figs, but they should be peeled first. It is perfect with crusty bread and butter, brioche or toast for breakfast, but would also make excellent jam tartlets or Italian *crostata*. There is a growing trend in the Veneto region of Italy to serve some of their more unusual cheeses with honey or fruit preserves.

Wipe the figs and chop into tiny pieces. Put in a saucepan with the lemon juice and 200 ml water. Cook over low heat until soft – this make take 20–30 minutes, but if the skins are not cooked until tender at this stage, they will be tough when boiled with the sugar. Add the sugar and cook over low heat until dissolved. Stir in the vanilla sugar, increase the heat and boil until setting point is reached (page 8), 5–10 minutes.

Take the pan off the heat and test for set. If the jam is not ready, put the pan back on the heat to boil for a few minutes longer and test again. Repeat this process if necessary and remember to take the jam off the heat while testing, because over-boiling will ruin it.

When setting point has been reached, skim the jam with a perforated skimmer, stir it well and let stand for 20 minutes for the fruit to settle. Stir and ladle into clean, dry, warm jars. Seal at once with waxed paper discs, wiping the necks of the jars with a clean, damp cloth if necessary. Close with a lid or appropriate cover. Let cool, label and store in a cool, dark cupboard until required.

VARIATION Try experimenting with peaches, nectarines and kiwifruit, though it may not be necessary to cook the fruit for so long.

1.5 kg firm black figs

freshly squeezed juice of 2 lemons

1.2 kg sugar

1 envelope of vanilla sugar, 7.5 g (optional)

3-4 clean, dry, warm jam jars, 250 g each, with lids or covers

waxed paper discs

MAKES 750 G-1 KG

Greengage jam

I love the combination of any plum and aniseed, whether for jam, chutney, bottling, stewing, pies, crumbles or fools. Cinnamon and cloves also work well if aniseed is not a favourite of yours, but do try it first. Greengages make a dark golden-yellow jam; other plum varieties will make jams that vary in colour from yellow to pink or purple.

1.5 kg greengages or other plums

1 large whole star anise

1.5 kg sugar

2-4 clean, dry, warm jam jars, 250 g each, with lids or covers

waxed paper discs

MAKES 500 G-1 KG

Rinse the fruit, remove the stalks and let dry naturally in the sun. Put the fruit in a large saucepan with the star anise and 100 ml water and simmer gently to soften the skins, taking care not to let the fruit become mushy.

Discard the star anise. Add the sugar and continue to simmer over low heat to dissolve the sugar, stirring all the time. Bring to the boil and remove as many stones as come to the surface. Boil rapidly until setting point is reached (page 8), 5–10 minutes.

If the jam is not ready, put the pan back on the heat to boil for a few minutes longer and test again. Repeat this process if necessary and remember to take the jam off the heat while testing, because over-boiling will ruin it.

When setting point has been reached, skim the jam with a perforated skimmer, stir it well and let stand for 20 minutes for the fruit to settle. Stir and ladle into clean, dry, warm jars. Seal at once with waxed paper discs, wiping the necks of the jars with a clean, damp cloth if necessary. Close with a lid or appropriate cover.

Let cool, label and store in a cool, dark cupboard until required.

VARIATION **Victoria plum jam**

If using large plum varieties such as Victoria, it may be a good idea to cut the plums in half and remove the stones before cooking.

Pineapple and apple jam

This jam is very refreshing and the prettiest shade of lemon yellow. If you are mad about pineapple, it could be good eaten straight off the spoon, Mediterranean style. Who needs bread? Try perking up some vanilla ice cream with a few spoonfuls of jam and a splash of rum. You could even paint a little rum on the inside of the wax seal before sealing the jars, just to give the jam a deliciously tropical taste.

1 kg pineapple flesh (2 fresh pineapples)

2 large cooking apples

freshly squeezed juice of 1½ lemons

about 1 kg sugar

8 green cardamom pods (optional)

3-4 clean dry, warm jam jars, 250 ml each, with lids or covers

waxed paper discs

MAKES 750 G-1 KG

If using whole pineapples, peel and core first. Cut out the 'eyes' with the point of a sharp knife or potato peeler. Peel and core the apples. Cut the pineapple and apples into tiny chunks. Weigh the fruit and transfer it to a large saucepan and sprinkle with lemon juice. Weigh 80 g of sugar for every 100 g of fruit and set aside. Add 150 ml water to the fruit and simmer over low heat until the apple softens, 20–30 minutes. Meanwhile, split open the cardamom pods, take out the seeds and crush them with a mortar and pestle. Add to the fruit as it cooks.

Add the weighed sugar to the pan and continue to cook over low heat until the sugar has dissolved, stirring all the while. Increase the heat and boil rapidly until setting point is reached (page 8), 5–10 minutes.

If the jam is not ready, put the pan back on the heat to boil for a few minutes longer and test again. Repeat this process if necessary and remember to take the jam off the heat while testing, because over-boiling will ruin it.

When setting point has been reached, skim the jam with a perforated skimmer, stir it well and let stand for 20 minutes for the fruit to settle. Stir and ladle into clean, dry, warm jars. Seal at once with waxed paper discs, wiping the necks of the jars with a clean, damp cloth if necessary. Close with a lid or appropriate cover.

Let cool, label and store in a cool, dark cupboard until required.

VARIATION Try experimenting with mangoes and other tropical fruit. Don't forget to add the apples, because they will help the jam set.

Rhubarb and ginger jam

This is a robust jam that deserves a place alongside the zingiest of marmalades. Choose young pink rhubarb if possible, because it will give lovely pink colour to the jam – green rhubarb tends to turn brown when cooked. However, the flavour is just as good whatever the colour. This would also make a delicious old-fashioned pudding such as jam tart, Bakewell tart, jam roly-poly or steamed jam pudding.

1.5 kg young rhubarb, pink if possible

1.5 kg sugar

grated zest and freshly squeezed juice of 1½ unwaxed lemons

30-45 g fresh ginger, peeled, to taste

3-4 clean, dry, warm jam jars, 250 ml each, with lids or covers

waxed paper discs

MAKES ABOUT 1 KG

Wipe the rhubarb, trim it, cut into chunks and put in a bowl with the sugar, lemon zest and juice. Cover and let stand overnight.

Crush the ginger with a mortar and pestle or blender and add to the fruit and sugar. Transfer to a large saucepan and bring slowly to simmering point, stirring all the time to dissolve the sugar. Simmer gently until the fruit has softened, then increase the heat and boil rapidly for 5–10 minutes until setting point is reached (page 8).

If the jam is not ready, put the pan back on the heat to boil for a few minutes longer and test again. Repeat this process if necessary and remember to take the jam off the heat while testing, because over-boiling will ruin it.

When setting point has been reached, skim the jam with a perforated skimmer, stir it well and let stand for 20 minutes for the fruit to settle. Stir and ladle into clean, dry, warm jars. Seal at once with waxed paper discs, wiping the necks of the jars with a clean, damp cloth if necessary. Close with a lid or appropriate cover.

Let cool, label and store in a cool, dark cupboard until required.

VARIATION **Blackcurrant and rhubarb jam**

Rhubarb combines well with soft fruit such as blackcurrants, raspberries and strawberries, giving them more body and reducing the seediness of the fruit. Use half soft fruit and half rhubarb, and omit the ginger.

Apple jelly with lemon and sage

My Brazilian friend Melodie is famous for her apple jelly, which she makes from windfall apples. She took me through the method from orchard to table in an animated monologue totally devoid of weights and measures or times.

1.5 kg apples (cleaned weight)

sugar or preserving sugar (see method)

freshly squeezed juice of 1½ lemons

a large bunch of sage or mint tied up tightly leaving a long piece of string free

a few extra sage leaves for decoration

a jelly bag or muslin

2-3 clean, dry, warm jam jars, 250 g each, with lids or covers

waxed paper discs

MAKES 500-750 G

Peel, core and chop the apples. Put them in a large pan and add enough water, so that if you peer in you can just see the water level appearing under the fruit. Part-cover with a lid and boil slowly until the fruit forms a pulp, 1–1½ hours.

Transfer the fruit pulp to a jelly bag suspended over a large bowl. (Melodie uses the legs of an upturned kitchen chair. I use an S-hook hung from a cupboard door.) Leave to drip all night. Do not be tempted to squeeze the bag, because this will make the jelly cloudy.

Measure the quantity of juice obtained. Pour it into a large pan. Add 450 g of sugar for every 600 ml of juice. Add the lemon juice. Set the pan over low heat and slowly dissolve the sugar, stirring all the while. When the sugar has dissolved, tie the bunch of sage to the handle of the pan and suspend in the jelly. Boil rapidly for 5–10 minutes until setting point is reached (page 8). Stir from time to time to make sure the pan does not burn.

If the jam is not ready, put the pan back on the heat to boil for a few minutes longer and test again. Repeat this process if necessary and remember to take the jam off the heat while testing, because over-boiling will ruin it.

When setting point has been reached, discard the sage and skim the jelly with a perforated skimmer. Stir the jelly and ladle into clean, dry, warm jars. Plunge a few fresh sage leaves into boiling water, pat dry and push one leaf into each jar. Seal at once with waxed paper discs, wiping the necks of the jars with a clean, damp cloth if necessary. Close with a lid or other appropriate cover.

VARIATION Other herbs such as rosemary and thyme and spices such as ginger, chilli, cinnamon or star anise can be used instead of the sage. If making chilli jelly, stir in 1–2 finely chopped, deseeded chillies instead of the bunch of sage.

Crab-apple jelly

If you have space for a small tree in your garden, it's worth planting a crab-apple. You will have pretty blossom in spring and jewel-like miniature apples in the late summer to early autumn. Use them to make this stunning pink jelly to serve with roast pork, poultry and game. Sadly, we don't have a crab-apple tree, but our friend Paul has two. One produces tiny scarlet and cream, plum-shaped fruit and the other a crimson, cherry-sized apple. This is his recipe.

1.5 kg crab-apples

1 unwaxed lemon

sugar or preserving sugar (see method)

a jelly bag or muslin

2-3 clean, dry, warm jam jars, about 250 g each, with lids or covers

waxed paper discs

MAKES 500–750 G

Sort the crab-apples, discarding any that are badly bruised or marked and any leaves that are still attached. Wash the fruit, cut them in half and put in a large saucepan. Fill the pan with water to just under the level of the fruit. Peel the zest thinly from the lemon and add this and the peeled lemon to the pan. Part-cover with a lid, bring slowly to the boil and simmer for 1 hour. Transfer to a jelly bag or muslin suspended over a large bowl and leave to drip all night.

Measure the juice into a clean preserving pan and, for every 600 ml of juice, add 450 g sugar. Set over low heat and bring to simmering point, dissolving the sugar, stirring all the while. When it has dissolved, increase the heat and boil hard for 5–10 minutes until setting point is reached.

Take the pan off the heat and test for set (page 8). If the jelly is not ready, put the pan back on the heat to boil for a few minutes longer and test again. Repeat this process if necessary and remember to take it off the heat while testing, because over-boiling will ruin it.

When setting point has been reached, skim the jelly with a perforated skimmer. Stir the jelly and ladle into warm, clean, dry jars. Wipe the necks of the jars with a clean, damp cloth. Seal at once with waxed paper discs, placed directly on top of the jelly. Seal the jars. Let cool, label and store in a cool, dark cupboard until required.

Red berry jelly

500 g strawberries

500 g raspberries or redcurrants

500 g loganberries or tayberries

500 g blackcurrants

freshly squeezed juice of 1 lemon

500 ml water

sugar or preserving sugar (see method)

a jelly bag or muslin

2–3 clean, dry, warm jam jars, 250 ml each, with lids or covers

waxed paper discs

MAKES 500-750 ML

Berries make a marvellous seedless jam – use sweet ones like strawberries and raspberries, blackberry-raspberry crosses like the Scottish tayberry or the Californian loganberry, then something sharp such as cranberries or red or blackcurrants. In season, every other farm gateway sets out 'pick-your-own' signs. Early summer is the time to enjoy these soft fruits fresh – and to make this jelly, which is delicious spread in the middle of a plain Victoria sponge cake or dissolved in boiling water for a warming winter drink.

Put all the fruit (no need to strip currants) in a large preserving pan with the lemon juice and water and bring slowly to the boil . Part-cover with a lid and simmer until the fruit has softened, 10–15 minutes. Transfer to a jelly bag or muslin suspended over a large bowl and leave to drip all night.

Measure the juice into a clean preserving pan and, for every 600 ml of juice, add 450 g sugar. Set over low heat and bring to simmering point, dissolving the sugar, stirring all the while. When it has dissolved, increase the heat and boil hard for 5–10 minutes until setting point is reached.

Take the pan off the heat and test for set (page 8). When setting point has been reached, skim the jelly with a perforated skimmer. Stir the jelly and ladle into warm, clean, dry jars. Wipe the necks of the jars with a clean, damp cloth. Seal at once with waxed paper discs, placed directly on top of the jelly. Seal the jars. Let cool, label and store in a cool, dark cupboard until required.

VARIATION Jelly made with redcurrants, blackcurrants or any single soft fruit.

Orange and kumquat marmalade

3 unwaxed sweet oranges, well scrubbed

115 g kumquats, well scrubbed

600 g sugar

freshly squeezed juice of ½ lemon

1 tablespoon honey

a jelly bag or muslin

2-3 clean, dry, warm jam jars, about 250 g each, with lids or covers

waxed paper discs

MAKES 500-750 G

Cut the orange zest into very thin strips with a sharp citrus zester. Put the zest in a large bowl and reserve. Cut away all the pith and put in a second large bowl.

Cut the orange into segments and reserve the segment skin, pips and central core of the orange, taking care to save any juice. Add the segments and orange and lemon juices to the bowl of zest. Add the reserved skin, pips and core of the orange to the bowl of pith.

Cut the kumquats in half lengthways, scrape out all the flesh, pith and pips with a teaspoon. Add this to the orange pith. Cut the kumquat 'shells' into thin strips and add these to the orange zest and segments.

Add 500 ml water to the bowl of fruit and add another 500 ml water to the pith and pips. Cover both bowls with a clean cloth and let steep overnight or for 24 hours.

Put the pith and pips in a pan and simmer, covered, over low heat for 30 minutes. Transfer to a jelly bag set over a bowl and let drain for 30 minutes. Squeeze the bag to extract the remaining liquid. You will notice that the juice on your hands is very sticky – this is the pectin extracted from the pith.

Pour the fruit, lemon zest and water into a large pan, then add the extracted liquid from the pith. Put over low heat, bring slowly to simmering point and cook until the zest softens and the liquid has reduced by half.

Add the sugar to the pan and bring slowly to simmering point, cooking and stirring until the sugar has dissolved. Because the sugar content is high, this will take quite a long time. When the marmalade has become translucent, you will know the sugar has dissolved and you can increase the heat. Bring to the boil and boil rapidly until setting point is reached, 5–10 minutes.

Take the pan off the heat and test for set (page 8). If the marmalade is not ready, put the pan back on the heat to boil for a few minutes longer and test again. Repeat this process if necessary and remember to take the pan off the heat during testing because over-boiling will ruin it.

When setting point has been reached, add the honey, return to simmering point, then turn off the heat. Skim with a perforated skimmer, stir well and let stand for 30 minutes for the fruit to settle. Stir and ladle into clean, dry, warm jars and wipe the necks of the jars with a clean, damp cloth if necessary. Seal at once with waxed paper discs and covers.

Let cool, label and store in a cool, dark cupboard until required.

VARIATION **Mandarin and lemon marmalade**

Use 6–8 mandarins and 1 extra lemon in place of the oranges and kumquats.

Chunky lemon, lime and grapefruit marmalade

The beauty of this marmalade is that it can be made in small quantities at any time of the year, not just when Sevilles are in season. I have given quantities to yield two or three jars, but if you want to make it in bulk, then simply double or triple the ingredients. Cut the peel to suit your taste – thick or thin by hand, chunky or fine using a blender.

1 unwaxed lemon

1 small unwaxed pink grapefruit

1 unwaxed lime

500 ml water

1 kg sugar

freshly squeezed juice of ½ lemon

3 clean, dry, warm jam jars, about 250 g each, with lids or covers

waxed paper discs

MAKES 500–750 G

Scrub the fruit and prise out any stalk ends still attached. Put in a pan and cover with cold water. Set over low heat and cook until tender – this will take 1½–2 hours. The fruit is ready when it 'collapses'. Lime zest is much tougher than other citrus peel, so you must make sure it is tender at this stage.

Transfer the fruit to a chopping board and leave until cool enough to handle. Cut in half, scrape out all the flesh and pips and add to the pan of water. Bring to the boil and simmer for 5 minutes. Cut the zest into strips as thin as possible, or put it in a blender and blend until chunky. Strain the water from the pips and flesh and return it to the pan, adding the chopped zest and the lemon juice. Discard the pips and debris.

Add the sugar to the pan and bring slowly to simmering point, stirring until the sugar has dissolved. Because the sugar content is high, this will take quite a long time. When the marmalade has become translucent,

you will know the sugar has dissolved and you can increase the heat. Bring to the boil and boil rapidly until setting point is reached, 5–10 minutes.

Take the pan off the heat and test for set (page 8). If the marmalade is not ready, put the pan back on the heat to boil for a few minutes longer and test again. Repeat this process if necessary and remember to take the pan off the heat during testing because over-boiling will ruin it.

When setting point has been reached, return to simmering point, then turn off of the heat. Skim with a perforated skimmer, stir well and let stand for 30 minutes for the fruit to settle, stir and ladle into clean, dry, warm jars and wipe the necks of the jar with a clean, damp cloth if necessary. Seal at once with waxed paper discs and covers.

Let cool, label and store in a cool, dark cupboard until required.

VARIATION **Seville orange marmalade**

Use 1.5 kg Seville oranges and multiply other ingredients by 3. This will yield about 8 jars.

A relish is a preserve for serving with meat or cheese. It is simple to make, delicious and puts the ready-made kind in the shade. This combination of fruit, spice and port is truly festive and adds colour and sparkle to roasts such as turkey and lamb, game dishes, baked ham and savoury pies. This quantity will make enough to see you through the festive season, but should you relish the idea of year-round culinary cheer, make it in bulk.

Cranberry relish with orange zest, cinnamon and port

2 cm cinnamon stick

6 whole cloves

250 g stripped fresh cranberries or redcurrants

peeled zest and freshly squeezed juice of 1 unwaxed orange

250 g sugar

1–2 tablespoons port

a small muslin bag with kitchen string

1 clean, dry, warm jam jar, about 375 g, with lid or cover

waxed paper disc

MAKES ABOUT 375 G

Put the cinnamon and cloves in a small muslin bag and tie up with kitchen string. Alternatively, use ¼ teaspoon ground cinnamon and a pinch of ground cloves.

Put the cranberries in a preserving pan with the zest and juice of the orange, the bag of spices and the sugar. Simmer over low heat until the sugar dissolves and the fruit starts to pop, then boil for 5 minutes, until setting point is reached.

Take the pan off the heat and test for set (page 8). If the relish is not ready, put the pan back on the heat to boil for a few minutes longer and test again. Repeat this process if necessary and remember to take it off the heat while testing, because over-boiling will ruin it.

When setting point has been reached, discard the spice bag, stir in the port, skim the relish with a perforated skimmer, stir it well and let stand for 20 minutes for the fruit to settle. Stir and ladle into a clean, dry, warm jar. Seal at once with a waxed paper disc and wipe the necks of the jar with a clean, damp cloth if necessary. Close with a lid or appropriate cover.

Let cool, label and store in a cool, dark cupboard until required.

PRESERVED FRUITS

Be sure to read Preserved Fruits Explained (page 9) before starting a recipe.

Layered summer fruits in grappa

Where I live, we are surrounded by wonderful strawberry fields and commercial orchards set in an undulating misty landscape. Picking your own fruit is not much cheaper than buying it ready-picked direct from a grower, but as my daughter says, 'Think of all the fruit you eat while you are picking!' (She should know – when they were small, I had to offer to weigh her and her brother, as well as our baskets, before we started picking our own.)

120 g strawberries

180 g sugar

120 g raspberries

120 g cherries

grappa, white rum
or brandy
(see method)

*1 preserving jar,
500 ml, with
appropriate lid
and seal*

MAKES 500 ML

Put a layer of strawberries in the jar and sprinkle with 60 g sugar. Add a layer of raspberries and another 60 g sugar. Add the cherries and the remaining sugar, then top up the jar with enough grappa or other spirit to cover the fruit. Seal with a lid. Extra fruit can be added to the jar when the level falls.

The jar need not be filled straight away, but reopened and added to as each new fruit comes into season. Top up each layer of fruit with half its weight in sugar and enough spirit to cover the fruit each time the jar is opened. Serve with ice cream or alone, as a special pudding.

Note Blackcurrants, blackberries and plums may also be added.

VARIATION **Layered 'white' fruits with brandy**

Instead of the berries and cherries, use gooseberries, whitecurrants, white cherries, grapes, apricots, greengages and peaches. Greengages and apricots may be cut in half first, and peaches sliced.

Peach halves in brandy with star anise

Peach halves in brandy are a classic, but all kinds of fruits can be preserved in this way. Whole peaches can also be bottled – leave the skin on and pierce the fruit to the stone with a cocktail stick before poaching. They look magnificent, but take up a lot of room in the jar and consequently are best packed in 1–2 litre jars. As with all pickles and preserved fruits, after the jar has been opened, they should be used straight away, so keep this in mind. This recipe makes a lovely present and the peaches are delicious served with ice cream or on their own as an after-dinner treat.

Put the peaches in a large bowl and cover with boiling water. Leave for 2 minutes for the skins to lift, drain off the water and pull off the skins. Discard the water. Cut the peaches in half and poach in plenty of simmering water for 1–2 minutes until just tender. Lift out the peach halves with a slotted spoon and drain on kitchen paper.

Measure 500 ml of the poaching water into a pan. Add 300 g of the sugar, dissolve over low heat, then bring to the boil and boil for 7 minutes. Don't forget to keep an eye on it.

When the peach halves have cooled, arrange them in a heatproof dish in a single layer, cover with the boiling syrup and leave for 24 hours.

After this time, pour the syrup off the peach halves into a saucepan and add the remaining 100 g sugar. Bring slowly to simmering point to dissolve the sugar, then boil for 2 minutes. Pour this back over the peaches, cool, cover with a cloth or lid and leave for 2 more days.

After 2 days, transfer the peach halves to a clean 500 ml jar.

Pour 200 ml of the syrup into a measuring jug and add to it an equal quantity of brandy. Pour the mixture over the peaches until covered, add the star anise on the outside of the fruit but on the inside of the glass and keep for at least 1 month before using. Label at once.

VARIATION Nectarine halves, plums, cherries and apricots can be prepared the same way but there is no need to peel them. Use a cinnamon stick or vanilla to flavour the fruit instead of the star anise.

4 firm just-ripe peaches

400 g sugar

200 ml brandy

1 whole star anise

1 preserving jar, 500 ml, with appropriate lid and seal

MAKES 500 ML

Pickled pears with tamarind and ginger

Pickled fruits such as these can be made with all kinds of vinegars; red and white wine, cider, perry or rice. I have used dark malt vinegar because, however careful you are, some varieties of pear turn brown when preserved. The flavour is not impaired, nor the texture of fruit, but the colour is a little off-putting. If you use dark malt vinegar, the change of colour goes unnoticed. When pickling peaches, figs, quinces and other more delicate fruits, I would suggest using white wine or other subtle vinegars. The combination of spices used in this recipe comes originally from the Middle East, but try others such as chilli, dill, allspice or coriander seeds. If you are not able to get hold of tamarind paste, simply omit it.

Put the vinegar, ginger, garlic, tamarind paste, cumin seeds, salt and sugar in a pan and bring slowly to simmering point. Cook over low heat until the sugar has dissolved, then boil for 5 minutes.

Meanwhile, peel the pears, cut in half and pack into the warmed jars. Fill to the brim with the reduced vinegar. If there isn't enough vinegar to cover the fruit, simply boil up extra vinegar, adding 40 g sugar to every 100 ml vinegar, and top up the jars. Seal the jars according to the manufacturer's instructions. Label when cold.

Keep at least 3 months before opening. Serve with cheese at the end of a meal, or as part of a cured meat starter, with cold cooked meats, hot gammon, hot game dishes or cold game pies.

Note Peaches and figs do not need peeling – pears and quinces do.

500 ml malt vinegar (see above)

35 g fresh ginger, peeled and finely grated

3 garlic cloves, crushed

3 heaped teaspoons of tamarind paste (available in Asian stores and some supermarkets)

1½ teaspoons cumin seeds

a pinch of salt

200 g demerara sugar

1 kg firm pears, peaches, figs or quinces (see note)

3 clean, dry, warm preserving jars, 500 ml each, or 1.5 litre jar, with appropriate lids and seals

MAKES 1.5 LITRES

LIQUEURS

B e sure to read Liqueur Making Explained (page 9) before starting a recipe.

Limoncello 'San Vigilio'

I was a guest at Villa San Vigilio on Lake Garda, which boasts a famous formal Italian garden (most received an 'English' makeover at the time of the Grand Tour). In this garden is a truly magnificent ancient lemon tree, so tall and so laden with huge fruit that the temptation to climb into it was overwhelming. Inspired by the sight of the wonderful tree, I was sure the family would have a recipe for Limoncello. Not so—and why should they? Garda is in the north of Italy and this is a drink from Campania. However, one of my hosts was from Naples and he promised to provide a recipe via his good friend, 'a fantastic Neapolitan cook, Fabrizia Gerli', and this is it.

4–5 unwaxed lemons, 1 of which should be greenish

500 ml clear spirits, such as gin, grappa, vodka or white rum

150 g sugar

1 wide-necked jar, 1 litre, with screwtop lid

1 funnel

1 bottle, 750 ml

1 coffee filter paper

1 cork

MAKES 750 ML

Remove all the lemon zest with a small sharp knife, making sure there is no white pith whatsoever. Put the zest in a large jar, then add the spirits of your choice. Cover with clingfilm and seal with a screwtop lid. Put in a dark place for 7–10 days, shaking the jar from time to time.

To make a syrup, put the sugar and 500 ml water in a saucepan and boil it for 6–7 minutes. Let cool. Pour the spirits off the zest and mix with the cooled syrup. (Discard the zest or cut it into fine strips, freeze and serve on sorbets and water ices, or in gin and tonic.) Put a funnel into the neck of the bottle and a coffee filter paper in the funnel. Carefully strain the liquor into the bottle, seal with a cork and put it back in the dark. It will be ready to drink after 1 week.

When the limoncello is ready to drink, it can be stored in the freezer – the alcohol content will stop it from freezing. Serve from the freezer.

Orange shrub

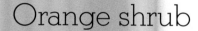

Of all the recipes in this chapter, shrub is the simplest to make. Traditionally it can be made with any kind of citrus fruit, so try experimenting with grapefruit, lime and lemon for a change. It is advisable to use unwaxed fruit, but not essential. Some shrub recipes contain wine, but the essential ingredient seems to be citrus fruit. Because there is always a ready supply of citrus, this is one drink that can be made whenever the spirit moves you, if you will forgive the pun.

700 ml white rum or brandy

finely grated zest of 2 unwaxed oranges and 100 ml juice

200 g sugar

1 wide-necked jar, 1 litre, with screwtop lid

1 clean, dry bottle, 1 litre

1 coffee filter paper

1 funnel

1 cork

MAKES 1 LITRE

Put the rum, orange zest and juice and sugar in the jar, cover with clingfilm and seal with a screwtop lid. Set aside for 30 days, label with the date as a reminder and shake 2–3 times daily.

After 30 days, strain into the bottle through a filter paper set in a funnel. Cork the bottle. It should be kept for about 3 months in a cool, dark cupboard, but is delicious served straight away. Keep in the refrigerator and serve chilled.

Kumquat and saffron rosolio

The combination of citrus and saffron creates a splendid golden hue that glows in the sunshine while the elixir is steeping. The colour alone is reason enough to make it – and if you can acquire some unusual bottles to put it in, rosolio makes an exciting gift. If you are not keen on grappa, use gin or some other colourless spirit. Do not use brandy or dark rum, because this will spoil the colour. Oranges or mandarins can be used instead of kumquats.

3–5 kumquats (50–60 g)

250 ml grappa

a good pinch of saffron threads

350 g sugar

2 large screwtop jars, 500 ml each

1 clean, dry bottle, 750 ml–1 litre

1 coffee filter paper

1 funnel

1 cork

MAKES 750 ML–1 LITRE

Cut the kumquats in half lengthways, scoop out the flesh and pips with a spoon, then scrape out all the pith. Discard everything except the kumquat 'shells'. Put these in a large jar. Add the grappa and saffron, then seal with a circle of greaseproof paper tied down with a rubber band.

Set the jar on a sunny windowsill for 8 days. Label with the date. Shake the jar once a day. Put the sugar and 360 ml water in another jar, cover with clingfilm and screwtop lid and leave at room temperature for 8 days, shaking it from time to time to dissolve the sugar. On the eighth day, mix the two liquids and let stand for 24 hours at room temperature.

Strain the liquid into a bottle through a coffee filter paper set in a funnel. Seal the bottle with a cork, then label and store.

Store in a dark, dry cupboard at an even temperature and forget about it for at least 12 months. When you are ready to try it, pour into your best decanter and serve over ice in beautiful glasses (or straight from the freezer).

Ginger and juniper liqueur

This comes originally from the Veneto region of Italy and can be made and flavoured with all kinds of seeds and spices. If you have problems finding juniper berries, try a health food shop. If using a brandy base, use a warm spice such as cinnamon or vanilla instead of juniper. This is a deliciously warming pick-me-up drink on a cold winter's day.

Peel the fresh ginger, chop it coarsely and put in a bowl. Add the juniper berries and crush with the end of a rolling pin until both are mixed and crushed to a coarse paste. Alternatively, use a mortar and pestle.

Transfer the paste to a large, wide-necked jar, add the grappa or brandy, cover with clingfilm, then seal with a screwtop lid. Let steep for 20 days at room temperature. Shake the jar from time to time. It's a good idea to label the bottle with the date as a reminder.

After 20 days, put the sugar and 200 ml water in a saucepan and boil for 5–6 minutes until thick and syrupy. Let cool. Mix the syrup and spirit. Pour into the bottle through a filter paper set in a funnel. Cork well or seal, label and store away from direct light in a cool (frost-free) cupboard for 12 months.

25 g fresh ginger

25 g juniper berries

500 ml grappa or brandy

200 g sugar

1 wide-necked jar, about 1 litre, with screwtop lid

1 clean, dry bottle, 750 ml

1 coffee filter paper

1 funnel

1 cork or seal

MAKES 750 ML

Country bounce

I was attracted to this recipe in an old American cookbook by the following instruction, 'Cheap rum at 75 or 50 cents a gallon serves equally as well as the best spirit for Bounce.' What better reason for making it.

Use cherries, damsons, plums, currants, sloes, bilberries, blackberries or elderberries and make sure your fruit is just-ripe – not under- or over-ripe – and never damaged.

Put the plums (including the stones) in a large bowl and pound with the end of a rolling pin. Alternatively, use a mortar and pestle.

Add the rum, cover and let stand for 1 week at room temperature. Transfer the fruit pulp to a jelly bag set over a bowl and leave overnight to drain. Measure the quantity of juice and add 350 g sugar for every 500 ml of juice. Mix well and transfer to bottles. Cork or seal.

Label and store in a cool, dark cupboard for about 12 months. Filter and serve in your best decanter.

2 kg plums, large ripe black cherries or similar fruit

1 litre rum

350 g demerara sugar for every 500 ml juice

a jelly bag

2 clean, dry bottles, 750 ml each

2 corks or seals

MAKES 1.5 LITRES

Hedgerow gin

This is a classic country liqueur that can be made with almost any berry or stone fruit. The beauty is that it can be made with the rich summer and autumnal pickings of a country walk. Wild damsons and sloes are particularly popular, but it can be made with elderberries, rosehips, blackberries or blueberries – in fact all the edible fruits you find in the hedgerows.

Pack the fruit, gin and sugar into the jar. Cover with clingfilm and seal with a screwtop lid. Label the jar, put in a dark, dry cupboard at an even temperature and forget about it for 1 year.

When you are ready to try it, pour the spirit off the fruit into your best decanter, discarding (or eating) the fruit.

Don't forget, the longer you keep the liqueur the better it tastes.

500 g fruit

500 ml gin

500 g sugar

1 clean, dry, wide-necked jar, 1 litre, with screwtop lid

MAKES 750 ML

PICKLES AND CHUTNEYS

Be sure to read Pickle and Chutney Making Explained (page 9) before starting a recipe.

Layered pickled vegetables

This colourful pickle is easy to prepare and makes a delicious present. It is tempting to keep it on show, but like most preserves it is best kept in the dark. Vary the choice of vegetables according to season and layer them according to colour. Try broccoli, cauliflower, green beans, aubergines, fennel, small onions and cucumber. If you prefer, cut the vegetables into small squares and florets and mix them up, rather than layering them. Serve as part of a mixed hors d'oeuvres with olives, cheese and cold meats or add to stir-fries and casseroles.

Wash or wipe the vegetables thoroughly. Cut the peppers into rings, first discarding the seeds. Cut the carrots, courgettes and celery into strips, about 4 x 1 cm.

Layer the vegetables in a colander set over a bowl, sprinkling salt on each layer. Put a weighted plate on top and let stand overnight covered with a cloth.

To make the brine, put 300 ml water in a saucepan, add the salt, vinegar, garlic and sugar. Bring gently to the boil, then remove from the heat, cover and let cool.

The following morning, put the vegetables in a colander and pour boiling water over them. Drain and dry thoroughly with a clean cloth.

Pack them into the jars in layers, starting with half the red pepper rings, half the celery, followed by half the orange pepper, half the courgettes, half the yellow pepper rings and finishing with the remaining celery and half the carrot. Top up each layer of vegetables with brine as you go. When the jar is full, insert the garlic, chilli and dill.

Top up the jars to the brim with brine. Check for air bubbles – tap the sides of the jars to bring them to the surface or slide a thin knife blade down the inside of the jars to release them. Seal. Leave for at least 1 week before using. Keeps for 6–12 months. After opening, the flavour of the pickles starts to deteriorate, so finish them straight away.

1 large yellow pepper

1 large red pepper

1 large orange pepper

2 young carrots

4 small courgettes

1 celery heart

1 garlic clove

1 fresh chilli

a sprig of dill or oregano

salt

brine mix

1 tablespoon salt

75 ml white wine vinegar

2 teaspoons sugar

2 clean, dry, warm jars with lids, 500 ml each. Choose jars that are tall and thin rather than short and wide.

MAKES 1 LITRE

VARIATION **Mediterranean vegetables in oil**

Instead of brine, top each layer with extra virgin olive oil and 1 teaspoon wine vinegar. Add blanched garlic, chilli and oregano and seal.

Moroccan preserved lemons and limes in salt

2 unwaxed lemons
and 2 unwaxed limes

4 tablespoons
coarse sea salt

freshly squeezed juice
of 1 lemon

a preserving jar, 500 ml

MAKES 500 ML

Lemons are preserved in salt in many Eastern cultures. In Morocco, they are preserved whole, slit in quarters almost to the base. As in all preserving, whole fruits require large quantities and large jars. As smaller pieces are easier to handle, I have adapted the recipe, cutting the fruit right through into quarters, but using the traditional Moroccan method, which is very simple and requires no cooking. Salted lemons and limes can be served with roasts and fish dishes, or put a piece of lemon inside roasting poultry and baste with the salty lemon juice. Chop them up small in rice or salads, or try experimenting with tequila cocktails.

Scrub the fruit well and remove the stalk base pieces with the point of a sharp knife. Cut the lemons and limes into quarters lengthways (taking care not to waste the juice) and put in a shallow bowl, cut sides up. Sprinkle half the salt onto the lemon flesh and let stand for 30 minutes.

Rub the salt into the fruit and pack into the jar, cut side down, pushing each wedge down well, alternating lime and lemon pieces. Top up each layer with the remaining salt. Don't worry if the jar is over-full, because the fruit will sink as the skin softens. Leave unsealed for 3–4 days, push the fruit down, top up with lemon juice and seal. Keep 1 month before use.

Winter's farm pickled onions

To my horror, I have recently discovered that we have no written record of our family recipe for pickled onions, made every autumn. I asked around – surely someone would have a tried-and-tested family recipe and, sure enough, I was told that 'Mary makes the world's best pickled onions'. However, like me, she had not made them recently and could not put her hand on the recipe. So this is a 'new' recipe based on the memory of two old ones.

60 g salt

500 g shallots or pickling onions

spiced vinegar

8 mixed peppercorns

4 whole cloves

1 cm cinnamon stick

1 cm cube of fresh ginger

400 ml malt vinegar

a clean, dry, warm 500 g jar with lid

waxed paper disc or greaseproof paper

MAKES 500 G

To make a brine, put the salt in a saucepan with 600 ml water. Bring to the boil, remove from the heat and let cool.

To peel the shallots, put them in a large bowl and pour boiling water over them for a few minutes. Drain and then peel.

Put the shallots in a bowl, add the cooled brine and leave for 24 hours. After this time, drain, rinse in cold water and dry carefully.*

To make the spiced vinegar, put the peppercorns, cloves, cinnamon and ginger in a small saucepan, add the vinegar, cover and bring to the boil over low heat. Turn off the heat, let cool, then strain.

Pack the onions into the jar, pushing them down with the handle of a wooden spoon. Top up with the cooled spiced vinegar.

Tap the sides to remove any air bubbles or slide a thin knife blade down the inside of the jar to release them.

Cover with a waxed paper disc or greaseproof paper, seal the jar and store in a cool, dark cupboard until required. Wait at least 3 months before tasting.

* If you would like sweet pickled onions, at this point put the onions in a bowl, sprinkle with 25 g demerara sugar and let stand for 24 hours, stirring from time to time to dissolve the sugar. Ladle some of the dissolved sugar into the jar with the onions before topping up with the vinegar.

Japanese pickled ginger

This is a very simple recipe for preserving fresh ginger. Traditionally, it is salted and cut into paper-thin rounds, preserved in rice vinegar and served with sushi and other Japanese dishes. I like to cut some of the ginger in rounds and some in julienne and layer it in small jars. The ginger julienne can be served mixed with a julienne of vegetables and citrus zests to serve with roasts, marinated fish dishes and all kinds of Oriental food. It is also very useful as a standby for adding to any recipe that requires fresh ginger.

175 g fresh ginger

1 heaped teaspoon salt

175 ml rice vinegar

30 g sugar

1 small, clean, dry, warm jar, with lid

MAKES 150 ML

Choose nicely rounded pieces of ginger root. Separate the root into 'lumps' and peel them. Rub the lumps with salt and leave in a covered bowl overnight.

Put the vinegar, sugar and 180 ml water in a bowl and stir to dissolve the sugar.

Slice the ginger as thinly as possible, blanch quickly in boiling water and dry on kitchen paper.

Fill a clean jar with ginger pieces and top with the vinegar marinade. Seal the jar. The pickle will be ready for use immediately and will keep well in the refrigerator after opening.

Note Ginger turns yellow when blanched and pink when pickled. If you have problems finding rice vinegar with the other vinegars, you'll find it near the sushi ingredients in the supermarket, or in a health food shop. Try using white wine vinegar or dry sherry instead.

Indian green mango chutney

1 onion (100 g) cut into quarters

2–5 green and red chillies (to taste), halved and deseeded

1 egg-sized piece of fresh ginger, peeled and cut into quarters

2 garlic cloves, peeled

30 g mixed mustard seeds

15 g cumin seeds

2 teaspoon ground turmeric

½ teaspoon salt

200 ml white wine vinegar

1 tablespoon olive oil

100 g sugar

600 g green mangoes or other under-ripe fruit, cut into 1 cm cubes

4 small, clean, dry, warm jars, 200 ml each, with lids or covers

waxed paper discs or greaseproof paper

MAKES 800 ML

This recipe is based on a traditional Indian pickle where the spices and onion are reduced to a paste, then cooked in vinegar. The sugar and fruit are added towards the end and simmered just for a short while. Hard green fruit is used traditionally, so try to find a hard mango rather than a ripe one. If ripe fruits are used, they will disintegrate too much and the idea is that the pickled fruit should retain its texture. Green or unripe papaya, peach, pear, quince and garden japonica can be also be used to make this recipe. Try preserving green beans this way too. The chutney goes well with spiced stir-fries and casseroles, roast meats, curries and Indian take-away. You could also try it with baked potato and scrambled eggs.

Put the onion, chillies, ginger, garlic, mustard and cumin seeds, turmeric and salt in a blender, add 2–3 tablespoons of the vinegar and grind to a paste.

Put the oil in a saucepan and cook the paste over low heat for 10 minutes, adding the remaining vinegar as the paste cooks down. Add the sugar and continue cooking over low heat until it has dissolved.

Add the fruit to the pan, stir well and simmer until just tender but not soft, about 10 minutes. Spoon the chutney into clean, dry, warm jars, cover with waxed paper discs or greaseproof paper, then seal. Let cool, label and store in a cool, dark place until required.

Grannie's apple chutney

My mother's chutney was renowned – so delicious that any other chutney paled into insignificance and still does. It was originally an old country recipe passed on to her by Mother Haywood, the elderly mother of the licensee of a local pub. A recipe is kept alive by a new owner and thus changes name. In her later years, we all called my mother 'Grannie' and so now it is her chutney. The best thing is, like most chutneys, it is very simple to make. Serve in pork sandwiches, with all kinds of eggs, cheese, cold meats or English breakfast.

Chop the apples and onions very finely – this can be done in a food processor, but take care not to reduce it a pulp. It is important for the chutney to have texture.

Put the apples, onions, raisins, sultanas, sugar, cayenne, mustard, ginger, salt and the 500 ml malt vinegar in a large pan and simmer for 1–1½ hours over low to medium heat. Stir regularly to make sure the sugar does not burn, adding extra vinegar as necessary as the chutney reduces.

Turn off the heat and let the chutney settle. Stir and pack into warm, clean jars, cover with a waxed disc and seal at once. Label when cooled.

Keep at least 1 month before you try it. This kind of chutney improves with age.

1 kg cooking apples, peeled and cored

500 g onions, quartered

125 g raisins

125 g sultanas

500 g demerara sugar

½ teaspoon cayenne pepper

½ teaspoon hot dry mustard

½ teaspoon ground ginger

25 g salt

500 ml malt vinegar, plus 500 ml extra to add as the chutney boils down

4-6 clean, dry, warm jars, 375 g each, with lids or covers, warmed in a low oven while the chutney is boiling

waxed paper discs

MAKES 1.5–2.25 KG

Pumpkin and red tomato chutney

There are many varieties of pumpkin and this recipe can be used to preserve all of them. Make sure that the flesh is firm and not stringy, or it will spoil the finished texture of the chutney. I like to cut the pumpkin by hand into 1 cm cubes, so it retains its colour and texture. If you are making large quantities, you may prefer to chop the vegetables in a food processor. You can also use other vegetables such as marrow, courgettes, aubergines, unripe melons and green tomatoes to make this recipe. Serve with a ploughman's lunch, scrambled eggs or cold meats.

Put the pumpkin, tomatoes, onions, sultanas, sugar, salt, ginger, garlic, nutmeg and the 200 ml vinegar in a saucepan and bring slowly to the boil. Simmer for 1 hour, stirring from time to time. The chutney should look dark, dense and rich. Top up with extra vinegar if the chutney dries out too much while cooking.

Transfer to the jar, cover the surface of the chutney with a waxed disc, wipe the jar with a clean, damp cloth and seal at once. Label when cool and store for 1–6 months in a cool, dark cupboard before opening.

400 g peeled and deseeded firm pumpkin or butternut squash flesh, cut into 1 cm cubes

200 g ripe tomatoes, skinned, deseeded and chopped

200 g onions, chopped

25 g sultanas

250 g demerara sugar

1 teaspoon salt

3 cm fresh ginger, peeled and finely chopped

1 garlic clove, finely chopped

a little freshly grated nutmeg

200 ml malt vinegar, plus 100 ml extra

1 clean, dry, warm jar, 500 ml, with lid or cover

waxed paper disc

MAKES 500 G

Williamsburg
sweet watermelon rind pickle

300 g watermelon rind

100 ml white vinegar

150 g sugar

5 whole cloves

1 cm cinnamon stick

1 cm piece of fresh
ginger, crushed

*a fluted or frilled
pastry wheel*

*a spice ball or muslin
bag tied with string*

*1 clean, dry, warm jar,
370 ml, with lid,*

MAKES 375 G

I was drawn to this old Virginian recipe simply because of the idea of turning those hefty wedges of peel left after a feast of watermelon into something delicious. It is a reminder of the very essence of all preserving; nothing was ever wasted if it could be turned into something delicious, something ready-made to keep in the larder to pep up otherwise dreary winter food. Imagine when there was no ready-made food at all – how welcome a jar of pickle would have been. The finished pickle is a lovely, soft, dark green and you may be surprised how much flavour watermelon rind has. Eat it with any cured, boiled or baked ham and try it with cheese. Or just eat it from the spoon.

Using the pastry wheel, cut the rind into tiny squares. Put in a bowl, add the white vinegar and 100 ml water, cover and let stand overnight.

Next morning, put the pieces of rind in a jelly bag or sieve and let drain for 2 hours or until quite dry. Discard the liquid. Transfer the fruit rind to a piece of kitchen paper to absorb any remaining moisture.

To make the syrup, put the sugar and 350 ml water in a saucepan. Put the cloves, cinnamon and ginger in a spice ball or tie in a muslin bag and attach it to the handle of the pan so the spices are suspended in the syrup. Heat slowly to simmering point to dissolve the sugar, then boil for 10 minutes. Add the melon rind and simmer for 3 minutes.

Scoop out the rind with a slotted spoon and put in the jar. Keep boiling the syrup until it has thickened, then pour it over the rind to fill the jar. Seal the jar at once, let cool, then label.

Store in a dark cupboard for 1 month before tasting – invert the jar from time to time to make sure the sugar does not crystallize on the bottom.

index